God made the world

BOOK 1

OLD TESTAMENT STORIES

LAMB BOOKS

Sight Reading

God Made the World

written by Tiffany Thomas
illustrated by Kellie Wheeler

CFI • An imprint of Cedar Fort, Inc. • Springville, Utah

HARD WORDS:

space, earth, night, animals

PARENT TIP: Choose one or two words for the child to read, with you reading the more difficult words. Each time you read through the story, have them read an additional one or two new words.

This is space.

God wants to make an earth.

Day 1
God makes the day and night.

Day 2

God makes the sky and the water.

Day 3
God makes dry land.

God puts plants on the land.

Day 4

God makes the sun, moon, and stars

Day 5
God makes the animals.

Day 6
God makes a man and a woman.

The man is Adam.
The woman is Eve.

God says all the things
He made are good.

Day 7
God rests after making the earth.

ISBN 13: 978-1-4621-4336-8

Published by CFI, an imprint of Cedar Fort, Inc. • 2373 W. 700 S., Springville, UT 84663
Distributed by Cedar Fort, Inc., www.cedarfort.com

Library of Congress Control Number: 2022940542

Cover design and interior layout design by Shawnda T. Craig

Printed in China • Printed on acid-free paper
10 9 8 7 6 5 4 3 2 1

HELP your child read while also learning about the interesting stories from the Old Testament. Build your child's confidence in reading with the entire LAMB BOOKS series as they progress through each book!

MORE BOOK SETS AVAILABLE IN THE LAMB BOOKS SERIES

NEW TESTAMENT STORIES

FIRST GRADE READING LEVEL
APPEALS TO PRE-K – FIRST GRADE

See cedarfort.com for more uplifting children's books.

EBOOK

CFI
AN IMPRINT OF CEDAR FORT, INC.

CEDAR FORT
Publishing & Media

WWW.CEDARFORT.COM
WWW.AUTHORTIFFANYTHOMAS.COM

Adam and Eve in the Garden

OOK
2

OLD TESTAMENT STORIES

LAMB
BOOKS
Sight Reading

Adam and Eve in the Garden

written by Tiffany Thomas
illustrated by Kellie Wheeler

CFI • An imprint of Cedar Fort, Inc. • Springville, Utah

HARD WORDS:
garden, tricks, family, leave

PARENT TIP: Have the child use a finger, craft stick, twig, or other item to point to each word as they read.

This is Adam and Eve.

Adam and Eve live in Eden.

Eden is a beautiful garden.

God tells Adam and Eve
to take care of Eden.

God tells Adam and Eve
to make a family.

God tells Adam and Eve
to not eat from this tree.

This is Satan.
He is bad. He tells lies.

Satan tricks Eve into eating from that tree.

God tells Adam and Eve to leave the garden.

Adam and Eve
have to work hard.

They have a big family.

The end.

This is not an official publication of The Church of Jesus Christ of Latter-day Saints. The opinions and views expressed herein belong solely to the author and do not necessarily represent the opinions or views of Cedar Fort, Inc. Permission for the use of sources, graphics, and photos is also solely the responsibility of the author.

ISBN 13: 978-1-4621-4336-8

Published by CFI, an imprint of Cedar Fort, Inc. • 2373 W. 700 S., Springville, UT 84663
Distributed by Cedar Fort, Inc., www.cedarfort.com

Library of Congress Control Number: 2022940542

Cover design and interior layout design by Shawnda T. Craig

Printed in China • Printed on acid-free paper
10 9 8 7 6 5 4 3 2 1

HELP your child read while also learning about the interesting stories from the Old Testament. Build your child's confidence in reading with the entire LAMB BOOKS series as they progress through each book!

MORE BOOK SETS AVAILABLE IN THE LAMB BOOKS SERIES

NEW TESTAMENT STORIES

FIRST GRADE READING LEVEL
APPEALS TO PRE-K – FIRST GRADE

See cedarfort.com for more uplifting children's books.

ALSO AVAILABLE AS AN EBOOK

CFI
AN IMPRINT OF CEDAR FORT, INC.

CEDAR FORT
Publishing & Media

WWW.CEDARFORT.COM
WWW.AUTHORTIFFANYTHOMAS.COM

Noah and the Ark

OK

LD TESTAMENT STORIES

LAMB
BOOKS
Sight Reading

Noah and the Ark

written by Tiffany Thomas
illustrated by Kellie Wheeler

CFI • An imprint of Cedar Fort, Inc. • Springville, Utah

HARD WORDS:

flood, animals, build, long

PARENT TIP: If you or your child begin to feel frustrated about reading, take a break. Or stop and say a prayer.

This is Noah.

Noah is a man of God.

The people are bad.

God will send a flood.

God tells Noah
to build an ark.

Noah builds an ark.

God tells Noah to put animals on the ark.

Noah and his family
get on the ark.

God sends the flood.

They are on the ark
for a long time.

God says no more big floods.

The end.

ISBN 13: 978-1-4621-4336-8

Published by CFI, an imprint of Cedar Fort, Inc. • 2373 W. 700 S., Springville, UT 84663
Distributed by Cedar Fort, Inc., www.cedarfort.com

Library of Congress Control Number: 2022940542

Cover design and interior layout design by Shawnda T. Craig

Printed in China • Printed on acid-free paper
10 9 8 7 6 5 4 3 2 1

HELP your child read while also learning about the interesting stories from the Old Testament. Build your child's confidence in reading with the entire LAMB BOOKS series as they progress through each book!

MORE BOOK SETS AVAILABLE IN THE LAMB BOOKS SERIES

NEW TESTAMENT STORIES

FIRST GRADE READING LEVEL
APPEALS TO PRE-K – FIRST GRADE

See cedarfort.com for more uplifting children's books.

EBOOK

CFI
AN IMPRINT OF CEDAR FORT, INC.

CEDAR FORT
Publishing & Media

WWW.CEDARFORT.COM
WWW.AUTHORTIFFANYTHOMAS.COM

LAMB BOOKS
Sight Reading

The Tower of Babel

OK

OLD TESTAMENT STORIES

LAMB
BOOKS
Sight Reading

The Tower of Babel

written by Tiffany Thomas
illustrated by Kellie Wheeler

CFI • An imprint of Cedar Fort, Inc. • Springville, Utah

HARD WORDS:

Babel, Heaven, repent, tower

PARENT TIP: Repeating the same books over and over again helps increase fluency and speed.

This is the city of Babel.

The people in Babel are bad.

The people want to go to Heaven.

They do not want to repent.

The people try to build
a tower to go to Heaven.

God is sad and
mad at the people.

God changes how the people talk.

Each person has
a new speech.

No one knows what anyone else says.

The people leave
the tower alone.

They never finish the tower.

ENGLISH - THE END
SPANISH - EL FIN
FRENCH - LA FIN
GERMAN - DAS ENDE
FINNISH - LOPPU
ITALIAN - LA FINE
SAMOAN - O LE FAAIUGA

This is not an official publication of The Church of Jesus Christ of Latter-day Saints. The opinions and views expressed herein belong solely to the author and do not necessarily represent the opinions or views of Cedar Fort, Inc. Permission for the use of sources, graphics, and photos is also solely the responsibility of the author.

ISBN 13: 978-1-4621-4336-8

Published by CFI, an imprint of Cedar Fort, Inc. • 2373 W. 700 S., Springville, UT 84663
Distributed by Cedar Fort, Inc., www.cedarfort.com

Library of Congress Control Number: 2022940542

Cover design and interior layout design by Shawnda T. Craig

Printed in China • Printed on acid-free paper
10 9 8 7 6 5 4 3 2 1

HELP your child read while also learning about the interesting stories from the Old Testament. Build your child's confidence in reading with the entire LAMB BOOKS series as they progress through each book!

MORE BOOK SETS AVAILABLE IN THE LAMB BOOKS SERIES

NEW TESTAMENT STORIES

FIRST GRADE READING LEVEL
APPEALS TO PRE-K – FIRST GRADE

See cedarfort.com for more uplifting children's books.

ALSO AVAILABLE AS AN EBOOK

CFI
AN IMPRINT OF CEDAR FORT, INC.

CEDAR FORT Publishing & Media

WWW.CEDARFORT.COM
WWW.AUTHORTIFFANYTHOMAS.COM

God Calls Abraham

[illegible]OK

OLD TESTAMENT STORIES

LAMB
BOOKS
Sight Reading

God Calls Abraham

written by Tiffany Thomas
illustrated by Kellie Wheeler

CFI • An imprint of Cedar Fort, Inc. • Springville, Utah

HARD WORDS:

Abraham, baby, promises, Isaac

PARENT TIP: Repetition is the key to learning and remembering new sight words. Your child may need to see a new sight word many times before they recognize and remember it.

This is Abraham and his wife Sarah.

They are a good man
and a good woman.

The people in their city are bad.

God takes away the food.

Abraham and Sarah leave to find food.

God blesses Abraham and Sarah with land.

Abraham and Sarah are sad.
They have no babies.

God promises Abraham
a big family.

Sarah has a baby.
She is 90 years old.

Their baby is named Isaac.

Abraham and Sarah are happy.

The end.

ISBN 13: 978-1-4621-4336-8

Published by CFI, an imprint of Cedar Fort, Inc. • 2373 W. 700 S., Springville, UT 84663
Distributed by Cedar Fort, Inc., www.cedarfort.com

Library of Congress Control Number: 2022940542

Cover design and interior layout design by Shawnda T. Craig

Printed in China • Printed on acid-free paper
10 9 8 7 6 5 4 3 2 1

HELP your child read while also learning about the interesting stories from the Old Testament. Build your child's confidence in reading with the entire LAMB BOOKS series as they progress through each book!

MORE BOOK SETS AVAILABLE IN THE LAMB BOOKS SERIES

NEW TESTAMENT STORIES

FIRST GRADE READING LEVEL
APPEALS TO PRE-K – FIRST GRADE

See cedarfort.com for more uplifting children's books.

EBOOK

CFI
AN IMPRINT OF CEDAR FORT, INC.

CEDAR FORT Publishing & Media

WWW.CEDARFORT.COM
WWW.AUTHORTIFFANYTHOMAS.COM

LAMB BOOKS Sight Readin

Abraham and Isaac

OK

OLD TESTAMENT STORIES

LAMB BOOKS

Sight Reading

Abraham and Isaac

written by Tiffany Thomas
illustrated by Kellie Wheeler

CFI • An imprint of Cedar Fort, Inc. • Springville, Utah

HARD WORDS:

Isaac, altar, obeyed, angel

PARENT TIP: Have your child read out loud, even if they can read all of the words by themselves.

This is Abraham.

Abraham is a man of God.

This is Isaac.

Isaac is Abraham's only son.

Abraham loves
Isaac very much.

God wants to know
if Abraham will obey.

God gives Abraham a test.

God tells Abraham to slay Isaac on an altar.

Abraham is sad but he puts Isaac on the altar.

An angel comes
and saves Isaac.

God is glad that
Abraham obeyed.

The end.

ISBN 13: 978-1-4621-4336-8

Published by CFI, an imprint of Cedar Fort, Inc. • 2373 W. 700 S., Springville, UT 84663
Distributed by Cedar Fort, Inc., www.cedarfort.com

Library of Congress Control Number: 2022940542

Cover design and interior layout design by Shawnda T. Craig

Printed in China • Printed on acid-free paper
10 9 8 7 6 5 4 3 2 1

HELP your child read while also learning about the interesting stories from the Old Testament. Build your child's confidence in reading with the entire LAMB BOOKS series as they progress through each book!

MORE BOOK SETS AVAILABLE IN THE LAMB BOOKS SERIES

NEW TESTAMENT STORIES

FIRST GRADE READING LEVEL
APPEALS TO PRE-K – FIRST GRADE

See cedarfort.com for more uplifting children's books.

ALSO AVAILABLE AS AN EBOOK

CFI
AN IMPRINT OF CEDAR FORT, INC.

CEDAR FORT
Publishing & Media

WWW.CEDARFORT.COM
WWW.AUTHORTIFFANYTHOMAS.COM

Joseph Is Sold

OK

OLD TESTAMENT STORIES

LAMB BOOKS

Sight Reading

Joseph Is Sold

written by Tiffany Thomas
illustrated by Kellie Wheeler

CFI • An imprint of Cedar Fort, Inc. • Springville, Utah

HARD WORDS:

Egypt, Joseph, jail, brothers

PARENT TIP: When your child is stuck on a word, do not say the word for them. Count to five in your head, then share a strategy to find it out. (Look at the picture, sound it out, etc.)

This is Joseph.

Joseph has 11 brothers.

Joseph gets a new coat from his dad.

Joseph's brothers are mad.

The brothers put
Joseph in a hole.

Men come from Egypt.

Joseph's brothers
sell him to the men.

Joseph goes to Egypt.

Joseph is a slave.
He works hard.

A man's wife tells a lie about Joseph.

Joseph goes to jail.

The end.

ISBN 13: 978-1-4621-4336-8

Published by CFI, an imprint of Cedar Fort, Inc. • 2373 W. 700 S., Springville, UT 84663
Distributed by Cedar Fort, Inc., www.cedarfort.com

Library of Congress Control Number: 2022940542

Cover design and interior layout design by Shawnda T. Craig

Printed in China • Printed on acid-free paper
10 9 8 7 6 5 4 3 2 1

HELP your child read while also learning about the interesting stories from the Old Testament. Build your child's confidence in reading with the entire LAMB BOOKS series as they progress through each book!

MORE BOOK SETS AVAILABLE IN THE LAMB BOOKS SERIES

NEW TESTAMENT STORIES

FIRST GRADE READING LEVEL
APPEALS TO PRE-K – FIRST GRADE

See cedarfort.com for more uplifting children's books.

ALSO AVAILABLE AS AN EBOOK

CFI
AN IMPRINT OF CEDAR FORT, INC.

CEDAR FORT Publishing & Media

WWW.CEDARFORT.COM
WWW.AUTHORTIFFANYTHOMAS.COM

LAMB BOOKS Sight Reading

Joseph Forgives His Brothers

OK

OLD TESTAMENT STORIES

LAMB
BOOKS
Sight Reading

Joseph Forgives His Brothers

written by Tiffany Thomas
illustrated by Kellie Wheeler

CFI • An imprint of Cedar Fort, Inc. • Springville, Utah

HARD WORDS:

king, sorry, forgive, extra

PARENT TIP: Check for understanding. After a few pages, ask the child what has happened in the story so far.

This is Joseph in jail.

Joseph is a man of God.

The king has bad dreams.

Joseph tells the king
the dreams are a sign.

There will be 7 years
with lots of food.

Then there will be
7 years with no food.

7

The king listens to Joseph.

Egypt saves the extra food.

Joseph's brothers ask for food.
They see Joseph.

Joseph's brothers say they are sorry.

Joseph forgives his brothers.
They are all happy.

The end.

ISBN 13: 978-1-4621-4336-8

Published by CFI, an imprint of Cedar Fort, Inc. • 2373 W. 700 S., Springville, UT 84663
Distributed by Cedar Fort, Inc., www.cedarfort.com

Library of Congress Control Number: 2022940542

Cover design and interior layout design by Shawnda T. Craig

Printed in China • Printed on acid-free paper
10 9 8 7 6 5 4 3 2 1

HELP your child read while also learning about the interesting stories from the Old Testament. Build your child's confidence in reading with the entire LAMB BOOKS series as they progress through each book!

MORE BOOK SETS AVAILABLE IN THE LAMB BOOKS SERIES

NEW TESTAMENT STORIES

FIRST GRADE READING LEVEL
APPEALS TO PRE-K – FIRST GRADE

See cedarfort.com for more uplifting children's books.

EBOOK
CFI
AN IMPRINT OF CEDAR FORT, INC.
CEDAR FORT Publishing & Media
WWW.CEDARFORT.COM
WWW.AUTHORTIFFANYTHOMAS.COM

LAMB BOOKS Sight Reading

Moses Leaves Egypt

OK

OLD TESTAMENT STORIES

LAMB
BOOKS
Sight Reading

Moses Leaves Egypt

written by Tiffany Thomas
illustrated by Kellie Wheeler

CFI • An imprint of Cedar Fort, Inc. • Springville, Utah

HARD WORDS:

Moses, slaves, prince, basket

PARENT TIP: Find a comfortable place to do your reading. Like the couch, the bed, or a soft chair.

This is Moses as a baby.

A bad man tries to
get rid of all babies.

His mom hides
Moses in a basket.

The queen finds
Moses and keeps him.

Moses grows up as a prince.

Moses is really the son of a slave.

All of the people
of God are slaves.

God tells Moses to tell
the king to let the slaves go.

The king says no.
God sends scary things.

The king is scared and lets the people go.

Moses and his people
leave Egypt.

The end.

ISBN 13: 978-1-4621-4336-8

Published by CFI, an imprint of Cedar Fort, Inc. • 2373 W. 700 S., Springville, UT 84663
Distributed by Cedar Fort, Inc., www.cedarfort.com

Library of Congress Control Number: 2022940542

Cover design and interior layout design by Shawnda T. Craig

Printed in China • Printed on acid-free paper
10 9 8 7 6 5 4 3 2 1

HELP your child read while also learning about the interesting stories from the Old Testament. Build your child's confidence in reading with the entire LAMB BOOKS series as they progress through each book!

MORE BOOK SETS AVAILABLE IN THE LAMB BOOKS SERIES

NEW TESTAMENT STORIES

FIRST GRADE READING LEVEL
APPEALS TO PRE-K – FIRST GRADE

See cedarfort.com for more uplifting children's books.

ALSO AVAILABLE AS AN EBOOK

CFI
AN IMPRINT OF CEDAR FORT, INC.

CEDAR FORT
Publishing & Media

WWW.CEDARFORT.COM
WWW.AUTHORTIFFANYTHOMAS.COM

LAMB BOOKS
Sight Reading

Moses and the Red Sea

OK

OLD TESTAMENT STORIES

LAMB
BOOKS
Sight Reading

Moses and the Red Sea

written by Tiffany Thomas
illustrated by Kellie Wheeler

CFI • An imprint of Cedar Fort, Inc. • Springville, Utah

HARD WORDS:

trapped, chases, walk, closes

PARENT TIP: At the end of the story, have your child act out what was read.

This is Moses.

Moses and his people leave Egypt.

The king is mad.
He chases them.

The people come
to the Red Sea.

The Red Sea is very big.

The people are trapped.

Moses raises his
hand over the sea.

The Red Sea parts.

The people can walk across the dry land.

The king tries to cross.

The Red Sea closes.

The end.

ISBN 13: 978-1-4621-4336-8

Published by CFI, an imprint of Cedar Fort, Inc. • 2373 W. 700 S., Springville, UT 84663
Distributed by Cedar Fort, Inc., www.cedarfort.com

Library of Congress Control Number: 2022940542

Cover design and interior layout design by Shawnda T. Craig

Printed in China • Printed on acid-free paper
10 9 8 7 6 5 4 3 2 1

HELP your child read while also learning about the interesting stories from the Old Testament. Build your child's confidence in reading with the entire LAMB BOOKS series as they progress through each book!

MORE BOOK SETS AVAILABLE IN THE LAMB BOOKS SERIES

NEW TESTAMENT STORIES

FIRST GRADE READING LEVEL
APPEALS TO PRE-K – FIRST GRADE

See cedarfort.com for more uplifting children's books.

ALSO AVAILABLE AS AN EBOOK

CFI
AN IMPRINT OF CEDAR FORT, INC.

CEDAR FORT
Publishing & Media

WWW.CEDARFORT.COM
WWW.AUTHORTIFFANYTHOMAS.COM

LAMB BOOK
Sight Readin

Moses and the Ten Laws

OOK
1

OLD TESTAMENT STORIES

LAMB
BOOKS
Sight Reading

Moses and the Ten Laws

written by Tiffany Thomas

illustrated by Kellie Wheeler

CFI • An imprint of Cedar Fort, Inc. • Springville, Utah

HARD WORDS:

idols, holy, people, thing

PARENT TIP: Give frequent praise, especially when they keep working on a difficult word.

I
II
III
IV
V
VI
VII
VIII
IX
X

This is Moses.
He is a man of God.

God gave Moses 10 laws
to tell the people.

Law 1: Only worship one God.

Law 2: Have no idols.

Law 3: Do not say God's name in a bad way.

Law 4: Make Sunday a holy day.

Law 5: Obey your mom and dad.

Law 6: Do not kill.

Law 7: Only love your own husband or wife.

Law 8: Do not steal or rob.

Law 9: Do not tell a lie.

Law 10: Do not wish you had other people's things.

ISBN 13: 978-1-4621-4336-8

Published by CFI, an imprint of Cedar Fort, Inc. • 2373 W. 700 S., Springville, UT 84663
Distributed by Cedar Fort, Inc., www.cedarfort.com

Library of Congress Control Number: 2022940542

Cover design and interior layout design by Shawnda T. Craig

Printed in China • Printed on acid-free paper
10 9 8 7 6 5 4 3 2 1

HELP your child read while also learning about the interesting stories from the Old Testament. Build your child's confidence in reading with the entire LAMB BOOKS series as they progress through each book!

MORE BOOK SETS AVAILABLE IN THE LAMB BOOKS SERIES

NEW TESTAMENT STORIES

FIRST GRADE READING LEVEL
APPEALS TO PRE-K – FIRST GRADE

See cedarfort.com for more uplifting children's books.

ALSO AVAILABLE AS AN EBOOK

CFI
AN IMPRINT OF CEDAR FORT, INC.

CEDAR FORT
Publishing & Media

WWW.CEDARFORT.COM
WWW.AUTHORTIFFANYTHOMAS.COM

LAMB BOOKS
Sight Reading

Joshua and the Wall

OK

OLD TESTAMENT STORIES

LAMB
BOOKS
Sight Reading

Joshua and the Wall

written by Tiffany Thomas
illustrated by Kellie Wheeler

CFI • An imprint of Cedar Fort, Inc. • Springville, Utah

HARD WORDS:
Joshua, Israel, fight, trumpet

PARENT TIP: Encourage your child to read aloud to other people, such as siblings and grandparents.

This is Joshua.
He is a man of God.

Joshua is very strong.

Joshua leads the people when Moses dies.

Joshua takes the
people to Israel.

Bad men were in control of Israel.

Joshua fights them
for seven years.

One city has a big wall.

Joshua marches around the wall with his army.

They march around the wall
seven times and blow trumpets.

The wall falls down.

Joshua has saved the city.

The end.

ISBN 13: 978-1-4621-4336-8

Published by CFI, an imprint of Cedar Fort, Inc. • 2373 W. 700 S., Springville, UT 84663
Distributed by Cedar Fort, Inc., www.cedarfort.com

Library of Congress Control Number: 2022940542

Cover design and interior layout design by Shawnda T. Craig

Printed in China • Printed on acid-free paper
10 9 8 7 6 5 4 3 2 1

HELP your child read while also learning about the interesting stories from the Old Testament. Build your child's confidence in reading with the entire LAMB BOOKS series as they progress through each book!

MORE BOOK SETS AVAILABLE IN THE LAMB BOOKS SERIES

NEW TESTAMENT STORIES

FIRST GRADE READING LEVEL
APPEALS TO PRE-K – FIRST GRADE

See cedarfort.com for more uplifting children's books.

ALSO AVAILABLE AS AN EBOOK

CFI
AN IMPRINT OF CEDAR FORT, INC.

CEDAR FORT Publishing & Media

WWW.CEDARFORT.COM
WWW.AUTHORTIFFANYTHOMAS.COM

Samson and His Hair

OK
3

LD TESTAMENT STORIES

LAMB
BOOKS
Sight Reading

Samson and His Hair

written by Tiffany Thomas

illustrated by Kellie Wheeler

CFI • An imprint of Cedar Fort, Inc. • Springville, Utah

HARD WORDS:

lion, woman, strong, worship

PARENT TIP: If the child feels overwhelmed, cover the following words so they only see one word. Do not cover the pictures.

This is Samson.

An angel tells his mom to never cut his hair.

God blesses Samson
to be strong.

Samson kills a lion
with his hands.

The people are bad.
They worship idols.

God wants Samson to fight the bad men.

Samson loved
a bad woman.

The bad woman
cuts Samson's hair.

Samson is not strong.
Samson is in jail.

His hair grows back
and he prays.

Samson is strong again and saves his people.

The end.

ISBN 13: 978-1-4621-4336-8

Published by CFI, an imprint of Cedar Fort, Inc. • 2373 W. 700 S., Springville, UT 84663
Distributed by Cedar Fort, Inc., www.cedarfort.com

Library of Congress Control Number: 2022940542

Cover design and interior layout design by Shawnda T. Craig

Printed in China • Printed on acid-free paper
10 9 8 7 6 5 4 3 2 1

HELP your child read while also learning about the interesting stories from the Old Testament. Build your child's confidence in reading with the entire LAMB BOOKS series as they progress through each book!

MORE BOOK SETS AVAILABLE IN THE LAMB BOOKS SERIES

NEW TESTAMENT STORIES

FIRST GRADE READING LEVEL
APPEALS TO PRE-K – FIRST GRADE

See cedarfort.com for more uplifting children's books.

ALSO AVAILABLE AS AN EBOOK

CFI
AN IMPRINT OF CEDAR FORT, INC.

CEDAR FORT Publishing & Media

WWW.CEDARFORT.COM
WWW.AUTHORTIFFANYTHOMAS.COM

LAMB BOOKS Sight Reading

Ruth and Her Mother-in-law

OK

OLD TESTAMENT STORIES

LAMB
BOOKS
Sight Reading

Ruth and Her Mother-in-law

written by Tiffany Thomas
illustrated by Kellie Wheeler

CFI • An imprint of Cedar Fort, Inc. • Springville, Utah

HARD WORDS:

Moab, Boaz, Naomi, faith

PARENT TIP: Have a special celebration the first time a child reads an entire book without help.

This is Ruth.
She is from Moab.

Ruth marries a man from Israel.

His mom is named Naomi.

Naomi teaches Ruth about God and Ruth has faith.

Ruth's husband dies.

His mom moves back to Israel.

Ruth goes with Naomi.

Ruth cares for Naomi and gets food.

A man named Boaz sees Ruth helping.

Boaz and Ruth marry each other.

King David is later born into their family.

The end.

ISBN 13: 978-1-4621-4336-8

Published by CFI, an imprint of Cedar Fort, Inc. • 2373 W. 700 S., Springville, UT 84663
Distributed by Cedar Fort, Inc., www.cedarfort.com

Library of Congress Control Number: 2022940542

Cover design and interior layout design by Shawnda T. Craig

Printed in China • Printed on acid-free paper
10 9 8 7 6 5 4 3 2 1

HELP your child read while also learning about the interesting stories from the Old Testament. Build your child's confidence in reading with the entire LAMB BOOKS series as they progress through each book!

MORE BOOK SETS AVAILABLE IN THE LAMB BOOKS SERIES

NEW TESTAMENT STORIES

FIRST GRADE READING LEVEL
APPEALS TO PRE-K – FIRST GRADE

See cedarfort.com for more uplifting children's books.

ALSO AVAILABLE AS AN EBOOK

CFI
AN IMPRINT OF CEDAR FORT, INC.

CEDAR FORT Publishing & Media

WWW.CEDARFORT.COM
WWW.AUTHORTIFFANYTHOMAS.COM

LAMB BOOKS
Sight Reading

Hannah and Her Baby

OOK 5

OLD TESTAMENT STORIES

LAMB BOOKS
Sight Reading

Hannah and Her Baby

written by Tiffany Thomas
illustrated by Kellie Wheeler

CFI • An imprint of Cedar Fort, Inc. • Springville, Utah

HARD WORDS:

year, temple, boy, prophet

PARENT TIP: Do not push a child to read so much that they develop reading fatigue.

This is Hannah.

Hannah is a good woman of God.

Hannah prays every year to have a baby.

Hannah does not have a baby.

Hannah goes to
the temple to pray.

Eli, a man of God, says
God will answer her prayers.

Hannah has a baby boy.

Her son's name is Samuel.

Hannah tells God that
He can have Samuel.

Samuel goes to live
at the temple.

God visits Samuel and calls him to be a prophet.

The end.

ISBN 13: 978-1-4621-4336-8

Published by CFI, an imprint of Cedar Fort, Inc. • 2373 W. 700 S., Springville, UT 84663
Distributed by Cedar Fort, Inc., www.cedarfort.com

Library of Congress Control Number: 2022940542

Cover design and interior layout design by Shawnda T. Craig

Printed in China • Printed on acid-free paper
10 9 8 7 6 5 4 3 2 1

HELP your child read while also learning about the interesting stories from the Old Testament. Build your child's confidence in reading with the entire LAMB BOOKS series as they progress through each book!

MORE BOOK SETS AVAILABLE IN THE LAMB BOOKS SERIES

NEW TESTAMENT STORIES

FIRST GRADE READING LEVEL
APPEALS TO PRE-K – FIRST GRADE

See cedarfort.com for more uplifting children's books.

ALSO AVAILABLE AS AN EBOOK

CFI
AN IMPRINT OF CEDAR FORT, INC.

CEDAR FORT
Publishing & Media

WWW.CEDARFORT.COM
WWW.AUTHORTIFFANYTHOMAS.COM

LAMB BOOKS
Sight Reading

David and the Giant

OOK
16

OLD TESTAMENT STORIES

LAMB
BOOKS
Sight Reading

David and the Giant

written by Tiffany Thomas
illustrated by Kellie Wheeler

CFI • An imprint of Cedar Fort, Inc. • Springville, Utah

HARD WORDS:
giant, fight, sling, Goliath

PARENT TIP: If the child struggles with blending consonants, try saying other words with those same blends. Example: brings, bread, brake, brown.

This is David.

David takes care of sheep.

There is a war and
David's brothers fight.

David brings food
to his brothers.

The bad men have a giant named Goliath.

Goliath is nine feet tall.

The army is
afraid of Goliath.

David is not afraid.
He has faith in God.

David slings a rock at Goliath and Goliath dies.

Everyone is happy.

David becomes king.

The end.

ISBN 13: 978-1-4621-4336-8

Published by CFI, an imprint of Cedar Fort, Inc. • 2373 W. 700 S., Springville, UT 84663
Distributed by Cedar Fort, Inc., www.cedarfort.com

Library of Congress Control Number: 2022940542

Cover design and interior layout design by Shawnda T. Craig

Printed in China • Printed on acid-free paper
10 9 8 7 6 5 4 3 2 1

HELP your child read while also learning about the interesting stories from the Old Testament. Build your child's confidence in reading with the entire LAMB BOOKS series as they progress through each book!

MORE BOOK SETS AVAILABLE IN THE LAMB BOOKS SERIES

NEW TESTAMENT STORIES

FIRST GRADE READING LEVEL
APPEALS TO PRE-K – FIRST GRADE

See cedarfort.com for more uplifting children's books.

EBOOK

CFI
AN IMPRINT OF CEDAR FORT, INC

CEDAR FORT Publishing & Media

WWW.CEDARFORT.COM
WWW.AUTHORTIFFANYTHOMAS.COM

LAMB BOOKS Sight Reading

Solomon Is Wise

OOK
17

OLD TESTAMENT STORIES

LAMB
BOOKS
Sight Reading

Solomon Is Wise

written by Tiffany Thomas
illustrated by Kellie Wheeler

CFI • An imprint of Cedar Fort, Inc. • Springville, Utah

HARD WORDS:

Solomon, wisdom, half, dream

PARENT TIP: Practice the "silent e" rule in words with and without the e (cut/cute, mat/mate, bit/bite, rot/rote).

This is Solomon, the son of King David.

God calls Solomon
to be the king.

Solomon has a dream about God.

In his dream God asks Solomon what he wants most.

Solomon asks to
be a wise king.

God is happy and
makes him wise.

Two moms fight
over one baby.

Each mom says
the baby is hers.

Solomon has a plan
to find the right mom.

He says to cut the baby in half.
The real mom says no.

The people see
Solomon's wisdom.

The end.

ISBN 13: 978-1-4621-4336-8

Published by CFI, an imprint of Cedar Fort, Inc. • 2373 W. 700 S., Springville, UT 84663
Distributed by Cedar Fort, Inc., www.cedarfort.com

Library of Congress Control Number: 2022940542

Cover design and interior layout design by Shawnda T. Craig

Printed in China • Printed on acid-free paper
10 9 8 7 6 5 4 3 2 1

HELP your child read while also learning about the interesting stories from the Old Testament. Build your child's confidence in reading with the entire LAMB BOOKS series as they progress through each book!

MORE BOOK SETS AVAILABLE IN THE LAMB BOOKS SERIES

NEW TESTAMENT STORIES

FIRST GRADE READING LEVEL
APPEALS TO PRE-K – FIRST GRADE

See cedarfort.com for more uplifting children's books.

EBOOK

CFI
AN IMPRINT OF
CEDAR FORT, INC.

CEDAR FORT
Publishing & Media

WWW.CEDARFORT.COM
WWW.AUTHORTIFFANYTHOMAS.COM

LAMB
BOOKS
Sight Reading

Elijah and Elisha

OOK
18

OLD TESTAMENT STORIES

LAMB
BOOKS
Sight Reading

Elijah and Elisha

written by Tiffany Thomas
illustrated by Kellie Wheeler

CFI • An imprint of Cedar Fort, Inc. • Springville, Utah

HARD WORDS:

Elijah, bathe, wicked, quiet

PARENT TIP: Explain that "q" almost always is paired with the letter "u" in a word.

This is Elijah.
He is a man of God.

A sick king visits Elijah.

Elijah tells the king to
bathe seven times in a river.

The king is healed.

Elijah uses fire to burn wicked men and idols.

The wicked people
are angry at him.

God sends Elisha
to help Elijah.

They learn God is
not in the wind.

God talks to them
in a quiet voice.

It is time for Elijah to die.

Elisha is the new prophet.

The end.

ISBN 13: 978-1-4621-4336-8

Published by CFI, an imprint of Cedar Fort, Inc. • 2373 W. 700 S., Springville, UT 84663
Distributed by Cedar Fort, Inc., www.cedarfort.com

Library of Congress Control Number: 2022940542

Cover design and interior layout design by Shawnda T. Craig

Printed in China • Printed on acid-free paper
10 9 8 7 6 5 4 3 2 1

HELP your child read while also learning about the interesting stories from the Old Testament. Build your child's confidence in reading with the entire LAMB BOOKS series as they progress through each book!

MORE BOOK SETS AVAILABLE IN THE LAMB BOOKS SERIES

NEW TESTAMENT STORIES

FIRST GRADE READING LEVEL
APPEALS TO PRE-K – FIRST GRADE

See cedarfort.com for more uplifting children's books.

ALSO AVAILABLE AS AN EBOOK

CFI
AN IMPRINT OF CEDAR FORT, INC.

CEDAR FORT
Publishing & Media

WWW.CEDARFORT.COM
WWW.AUTHORTIFFANYTHOMAS.COM

LAMB BOOKS
Sight Reading

Esther and the King

OOK
9

OLD TESTAMENT STORIES

LAMB
BOOKS
Sight Reading

Esther and the King

written by Tiffany Thomas
illustrated by Kellie Wheeler

CFI • An imprint of Cedar Fort, Inc. • Springville, Utah

HARD WORDS:

Jew, queen, Esther, pretty

PARENT TIP: There are many double letters in this story: pretty, marry, all. Point out that your child does not have to say the letter two times.

This is Esther.
She is a Jew.

Esther is a woman of God.

Esther is very pretty.

The king wants
to marry Esther.

Esther is now a queen.

A bad man wants
to slay all the jews.

Esther wants to tell
the king but she is afraid.

Esther fasts and prays.
God helps Esther be brave.

Esther tells the king
she does not want to die.

The king saves Esther and all the jews.

The bad man dies.

The end.

ISBN 13: 978-1-4621-4336-8

Published by CFI, an imprint of Cedar Fort, Inc. • 2373 W. 700 S., Springville, UT 84663
Distributed by Cedar Fort, Inc., www.cedarfort.com

Library of Congress Control Number: 2022940542

Cover design and interior layout design by Shawnda T. Craig

Printed in China • Printed on acid-free paper
10 9 8 7 6 5 4 3 2 1

HELP your child read while also learning about the interesting stories from the Old Testament. Build your child's confidence in reading with the entire LAMB BOOKS series as they progress through each book!

MORE BOOK SETS
AVAILABLE IN THE
LAMB BOOKS SERIES

NEW TESTAMENT STORIES

FIRST GRADE READING LEVEL
APPEALS TO PRE-K – FIRST GRADE

See cedarfort.com for more uplifting children's books.

EBOOK

CFI
AN IMPRINT OF
CEDAR FORT, INC.

CEDAR FORT
Publishing & Media

WWW.CEDARFORT.COM
WWW.AUTHORTIFFANYTHOMAS.COM

LAMB
BOOKS
Sight Reading

Job Trusts God

BOOK 20

OLD TESTAMENT STORIES

LAMB BOOKS

Sight Reading

Job Trusts God

written by Tiffany Thomas
illustrated by Kellie Wheeler

CFI • An imprint of Cedar Fort, Inc. • Springville, Utah

HARD WORDS:

daughter, easy, devil, curse

PARENT TIP: Point out that two, too, and to are three different words that sound the same, but each different meaning has a different spelling.

This is Job.
Job is a man of God.

Job has seven sons
and three daughters.

Job has a lot of animals.

Job has a lot of faith.

Faith

Satan says Job has an easy life.

God lets the devil
give a test to Job.

All of Job's family dies.

All of Job's animals die, too.

Job gets very sick.

Job's wife tells
him to curse God.

Job does not curse God.
Job is blessed.

The end.

ISBN 13: 978-1-4621-4336-8

Published by CFI, an imprint of Cedar Fort, Inc. • 2373 W. 700 S., Springville, UT 84663
Distributed by Cedar Fort, Inc., www.cedarfort.com

Library of Congress Control Number: 2022940542

Cover design and interior layout design by Shawnda T. Craig

Printed in China • Printed on acid-free paper
10 9 8 7 6 5 4 3 2 1

HELP your child read while also learning about the interesting stories from the Old Testament. Build your child's confidence in reading with the entire LAMB BOOKS series as they progress through each book!

MORE BOOK SETS AVAILABLE IN THE LAMB BOOKS SERIES

NEW TESTAMENT STORIES

FIRST GRADE READING LEVEL
APPEALS TO PRE-K – FIRST GRADE

See cedarfort.com for more uplifting children's books.

ALSO AVAILABLE AS AN EBOOK

CFI
AN IMPRINT OF CEDAR FORT, INC.

CEDAR FORT
Publishing & Media

WWW.CEDARFORT.COM
WWW.AUTHORTIFFANYTHOMAS.COM

LAMB BOOKS
Sight Reading

Daniel and His Friends

BOOK 21

OLD TESTAMENT STORIES

LAMB BOOKS

Sight Reading

Daniel and His Friends

written by Tiffany Thomas
illustrated by Kellie Wheeler

CFI • An imprint of Cedar Fort, Inc. • Springville, Utah

HARD WORDS:

Palace, servant, three, court

PARENT TIP: The illustrations on each page will help your child understand and learn the words.

This is Daniel.
He is a good man.

Daniel has three friends.

The king wants the
four boys at court.

Daniel and his friends
come to the palace.

The servants tell them to eat bad foods.

Daniel and his friends want healthy foods.

The servants let them
eat healthy foods.

They eat healthy food
for three years.

The four boys are
the healthiest.

The king is happy.

The boys join the king at court.

The end.

ISBN 13: 978-1-4621-4336-8

Published by CFI, an imprint of Cedar Fort, Inc. • 2373 W. 700 S., Springville, UT 84663
Distributed by Cedar Fort, Inc., www.cedarfort.com

Library of Congress Control Number: 2022940542

Cover design and interior layout design by Shawnda T. Craig

Printed in China • Printed on acid-free paper
10 9 8 7 6 5 4 3 2 1

HELP your child read while also learning about the interesting stories from the Old Testament. Build your child's confidence in reading with the entire LAMB BOOKS series as they progress through each book!

MORE BOOK SETS AVAILABLE IN THE LAMB BOOKS SERIES

NEW TESTAMENT STORIES

FIRST GRADE READING LEVEL
APPEALS TO PRE-K – FIRST GRADE

See cedarfort.com for more uplifting children's books.

ALSO AVAILABLE AS AN EBOOK

CFI
AN IMPRINT OF CEDAR FORT, INC.

CEDAR FORT
Publishing & Media

WWW.CEDARFORT.COM
WWW.AUTHORTIFFANYTHOMAS.COM

LAMB BOOKS
Sight Reading

Daniel's Friends in the Fire

BOOK 22

OLD TESTAMENT STORIES

LAMB BOOKS

Sight Reading

Daniel's Friends in the Fire

written by Tiffany Thomas
illustrated by Kellie Wheeler

CFI • An imprint of Cedar Fort, Inc. • Springville, Utah

HARD WORDS:
fourth, angel, person, idol

PARENT TIP: Point out spaces between words and all of the different punctuation marks.

These are Daniel's three friends.

They live at court
with the king.

The king is not a man of God.

The king builds an idol.

The king says, "All the people will bow down to the idol."

Will the boys pray to the idol?
No, they won't.

The king is mad at
the three boys.

The king puts all three boys in a big fire!

There are four people in the fire!

The fourth person is
an angel from God.

The boys are saved by God and are not burned.

The end.

ISBN 13: 978-1-4621-4336-8

Published by CFI, an imprint of Cedar Fort, Inc. • 2373 W. 700 S., Springville, UT 84663
Distributed by Cedar Fort, Inc., www.cedarfort.com

Library of Congress Control Number: 2022940542

Cover design and interior layout design by Shawnda T. Craig

Printed in China • Printed on acid-free paper
10 9 8 7 6 5 4 3 2 1

HELP your child read while also learning about the interesting stories from the Old Testament. Build your child's confidence in reading with the entire LAMB BOOKS series as they progress through each book!

MORE BOOK SETS AVAILABLE IN THE LAMB BOOKS SERIES

NEW TESTAMENT STORIES

FIRST GRADE READING LEVEL
APPEALS TO PRE-K – FIRST GRADE

See cedarfort.com for more uplifting children's books.

ALSO AVAILABLE AS AN EBOOK

CFI
AN IMPRINT OF CEDAR FORT, INC

CEDAR FORT Publishing & Media

WWW.CEDARFORT.COM

WWW.AUTHORTIFFANYTHOMAS.COM

LAMB BOOKS Sight Reading

Daniel and the Lions

BOOK 23

OLD TESTAMENT STORIES

LAMB BOOKS

Sight Reading

Daniel and the Lions

written by Tiffany Thomas
illustrated by Kellie Wheeler

CFI • An imprint of Cedar Fort, Inc. • Springville, Utah

HARD WORDS:

trick, law, anyway, every

PARENT TIP: Explain that "some" does not use the silent e rule. Another exception is "come."

This is Daniel.

Daniel is friends with the king.

The king is not a man of God.

Daniel prays every day to God.

Some bad men hate Daniel.

They trick the king
into making a new law.

The people must pray to the king.

Daniel prays to God anyway.

The king puts Daniel in the lion's den.

God sends an angel
to keep Daniel safe.

The happy king lets Daniel out.

The end.

ISBN 13: 978-1-4621-4336-8

Published by CFI, an imprint of Cedar Fort, Inc. • 2373 W. 700 S., Springville, UT 84663
Distributed by Cedar Fort, Inc., www.cedarfort.com

Library of Congress Control Number: 2022940542

Cover design and interior layout design by Shawnda T. Craig

Printed in China • Printed on acid-free paper
10 9 8 7 6 5 4 3 2 1

HELP your child read while also learning about the interesting stories from the Old Testament. Build your child's confidence in reading with the entire LAMB BOOKS series as they progress through each book!

MORE BOOK SETS AVAILABLE IN THE LAMB BOOKS SERIES

NEW TESTAMENT STORIES

FIRST GRADE READING LEVEL
APPEALS TO PRE-K – FIRST GRADE

See cedarfort.com for more uplifting children's books.

Jonah and the Big Fish

BOOK 24

LAMB BOOKS

Sight Reading

OLD TESTAMENT STORIES

Jonah and the Big Fish

written by Tiffany Thomas
illustrated by Kellie Wheeler

CFI • An imprint of Cedar Fort, Inc. • Springville, Utah

HARD WORDS:

Fish, Jonah, storm, repent

PARENT TIP: "sh" can be difficult for younger children to pronounce. Allow them to develop at their own pace for a little bit.

This is Jonah.
He is a man of God.

The people in this city are bad.

God calls Jonah to
teach the bad people.

Jonah is afraid.
He runs away to a boat.

God sends a big storm.

Jonah tells the sailors
to throw him into the sea.

A big fish swallows Jonah.

Jonah is in the fish
for three days.

The fish spits Jonah out.

Jonah teaches the people.

The people repent
and are now good.

The end.

ISBN 13: 978-1-4621-4336-8

Published by CFI, an imprint of Cedar Fort, Inc. • 2373 W. 700 S., Springville, UT 84663
Distributed by Cedar Fort, Inc., www.cedarfort.com

Library of Congress Control Number: 2022940542

Cover design and interior layout design by Shawnda T. Craig

Printed in China • Printed on acid-free paper
10 9 8 7 6 5 4 3 2 1

HELP your child read while also learning about the interesting stories from the Old Testament. Build your child's confidence in reading with the entire LAMB BOOKS series as they progress through each book!

MORE BOOK SETS AVAILABLE IN THE LAMB BOOKS SERIES

NEW TESTAMENT STORIES

FIRST GRADE READING LEVEL
APPEALS TO PRE-K – FIRST GRADE

See cedarfort.com for more uplifting children's books.

EBOOK

CFI
AN IMPRINT OF CEDAR FORT INC

CEDAR FORT
Publishing & Media

WWW.CEDARFORT.COM
WWW.AUTHORTIFFANYTHOMAS.COM

LAMB BOOKS
Sight Reading

Isaiah Sees Jesus

BOOK 25

OLD TESTAMENT STORIES

LAMB BOOKS

Sight Reading

Isaiah Sees Jesus

written by Tiffany Thomas
illustrated by Kellie Wheeler

CFI • An imprint of Cedar Fort, Inc. • Springville, Utah

HARD WORDS:

stable, second, Isaiah, future

PARENT TIP: Words that begin with "wh" can be tricky. Instead of sounding them out, have them become sight words to memorize.

This is the prophet Isaiah.

Isaiah is a man of God.

Isaiah was the prophet
for four kings.

God shows Isaiah the future.

Isaiah sees when Jesus is born.

Jesus will be born in a stable.

Jesus will die for our sins.

Isaiah sees the Second Coming.

God has Isaiah tell
the people about Jesus.

The people did not want to hear Isaiah.

Isaiah wrote down what he saw.

The end.

ISBN 13: 978-1-4621-4336-8

Published by CFI, an imprint of Cedar Fort, Inc. • 2373 W. 700 S., Springville, UT 84663
Distributed by Cedar Fort, Inc., www.cedarfort.com

Library of Congress Control Number: 2022940542

Cover design and interior layout design by Shawnda T. Craig

Printed in China • Printed on acid-free paper
10 9 8 7 6 5 4 3 2 1

HELP your child read while also learning about the interesting stories from the Old Testament. Build your child's confidence in reading with the entire LAMB BOOKS series as they progress through each book!

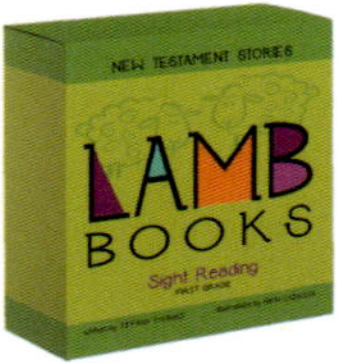

MORE BOOK SETS
AVAILABLE IN THE
LAMB BOOKS SERIES

NEW TESTAMENT STORIES

FIRST GRADE READING LEVEL
APPEALS TO PRE-K – FIRST GRADE

See cedarfort.com for more uplifting children's books.

ALSO AVAILABLE AS AN EBOOK

CFI
AN IMPRINT OF CEDAR FORT, INC.

CEDAR FORT
Publishing & Media

WWW.CEDARFORT.COM
WWW.AUTHORTIFFANYTHOMAS.COM

LAMB BOOKS
Sight Reading